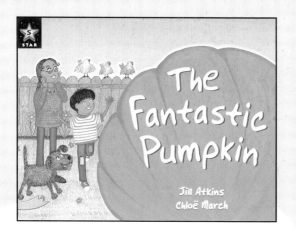

Walkth...

Let's read the title together.

Why is the pumpkin fantastic?

What does fantastic mean?

Do you know any other stories with 'fantastic' in the title? (e.g. *'Fantastic Mr Fox'* by *Roald Dahl*.)

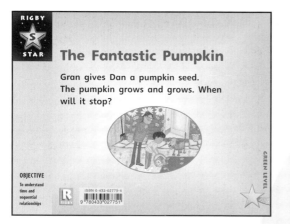

Walkthrough

Let's read the blurb together.

How big do you think the pumpkin will grow?

Walkthrough

Let's read the title again.

These are the author's and illustrator's names.

This is the publisher's logo.

Walkthrough

What did Grandma tell Dan to do with the seed?

Does Dan know what it will grow into?

How can you tell?

Grandma gave Dan a seed.
"What will grow from this seed?" said Dan.
"Plant it in my garden," said Grandma,
"and we will see!"

2

 Observe and Prompt

Check the children understand the speech marks, question mark and exclamation mark, and read with appropriate expression, pace and fluency.

Walkthrough

What did Dan do with the seed?

Dan planted the seed in Grandma's garden.

3

Observe and Prompt

Check the children read the 'ed' ending on 'planted' and the final 's' on 'Grandma's'.

Walkthrough

What did Dan do every day?

He watered the seed every day.

4

👁 **Observe and Prompt**

Check the children use picture cues for 'watered'.

Check they can read 'every'; if necessary, ask them to re-read the sentence and think of the best-fit word.

Dan looked in the garden every day.
"When will it grow?" he said.

5

 Observe and Prompt

Check the children read with expression, taking notice of the punctuation.

Walkthrough

What has helped the pumpkin grow?

What can Dan see?

What does Dan say?

The sun shone and the rain fell.
Then one day, Dan saw a little plant.
"Look!" he said. "It's a pumpkin!"

6

 Observe and Prompt

If a child cannot read 'shone', ask him/her to look at the first two letters 'sh' and sound out the phoneme. Then ask the child to read to the end of the sentence, then to re-run the sentence, filling in the word that makes sense.

Walkthrough

What happened the next day?

The sun shone and the rain fell.
The next day, the pumpkin was a little bigger.

7

 Observe and Prompt

Check the children can read with pace and fluency.

Check the children notice the repetitive pattern
'The sun shone ...'

Walkthrough

How big is the pumpkin now?

The sun shone and the rain fell
and the pumpkin grew and grew.
"It's as big as my football," said Dan.

8

Observe and Prompt

Check the children notice the repeating pattern
'The sun shone …'

If a child cannot read 'football', ask him/her to cross-check the
picture and the initial letter.

The pumpkin **grew bigger**.
"It's as big as my bicycle," said Dan.

9

Observe and Prompt

Check the children read with expression appropriate to the enlarged bold type.

Walkthrough

What is it as big as now?

Why do you think people have come to see the pumpkin?

It grew bigger.

"It's as big as you," said Grandma.

10

Observe and Prompt

Check the children read bold type with expression.

How big do these people think it is?

Some people came to see it.
"It's as big as our car!" they said.

11

 Observe and Prompt

Check the children can read 'people'; if necessary, prompt them to look at the picture for a clue.

Walkthrough

How big does this man think it is?

Do you think it can grow much bigger?

It grew bigger.

"It's as big as my van!" said a man.

12

Observe the children read the bold type with expression.

Walkthrough

Where have these people come from?

Why have they come?

What do they think of the pumpkin?

What do you think might happen if the pumpkin grows bigger?

Some people from television came to see it.
"What a fantastic pumpkin!" they said.

13

👁 Observe and Prompt

Check the children read with expression appropriate to the punctuation.

More and more people came to see it.
"It's as big as a house!" they said.

14

⬤ **Observe and Prompt**

Check the children can read 'more'; if necessary, refer them back to page 11 and say, 'Some people came to look, now there are …'

Walkthrough

What happened to the pumpkin?

What do you think they can do with it?

Then one day the pumpkin stopped growing – just like that!
"What can they do with it?"
asked the people.

15

Observe and Prompt

Check the children read 'asked'; if a child reads 'said', ask him/her to look at the initial letter and think of a word similar to 'said'.

Walkthrough

Were you right?

What did Dan make out of it?

What did he call the playhouse?

Can you find the word 'fantastic'?

"It's a **fantastic** playhouse!" said Dan.

16

👁 Observe and Prompt

Observe children read the bold type with expression.